zombies coloring book

Speedy Publishing LLC
40 E. Main St. #1156
Newark, DE 19711

www.speedypublishing.com

Copyright 2014
9781634286060
First Printed August 26, 2014

this book belongs to

_____

Add some colors to the picture by copying the colors from the next page!

Look at the colors! Make the pictures look the same by copying the colors!

Add some colors to the picture by copying the colors from the next page!

Look at the colors! Make the pictures look the same by copying the colors!

Add some colors to the picture by copying the colors from the next page!

Look at the colors! Make the pictures look the same by copying the colors!

Add some colors to the picture by copying the colors from the next page!

Look at the colors! Make the pictures look the same by copying the colors!

Add some colors to the picture by copying the colors from the next page!

Look at the colors! Make the pictures look the same by copying the colors!

Add some colors to the picture by copying the colors from the next page!

Look at the colors! Make the pictures look the same by copying the colors!

Add some colors to the picture by copying the colors from the next page!

Look at the colors! Make the pictures look the same by copying the colors!

Add some colors to the picture by copying the colors from the next page!

Look at the colors! Make the pictures look the same by copying the colors!

Add some colors to the picture by copying the colors from the next page!

Look at the colors! Make the pictures look the same by copying the colors!

Add some colors to the picture by copying the colors from the next page!

Look at the colors! Make the pictures look the same by copying the colors!

Add some colors to the picture by copying the colors from the next page!

Look at the colors! Make the pictures look the same by copying the colors!

Add some colors to the picture by copying the colors from the next page!

Look at the colors! Make the pictures look the same by copying the colors!

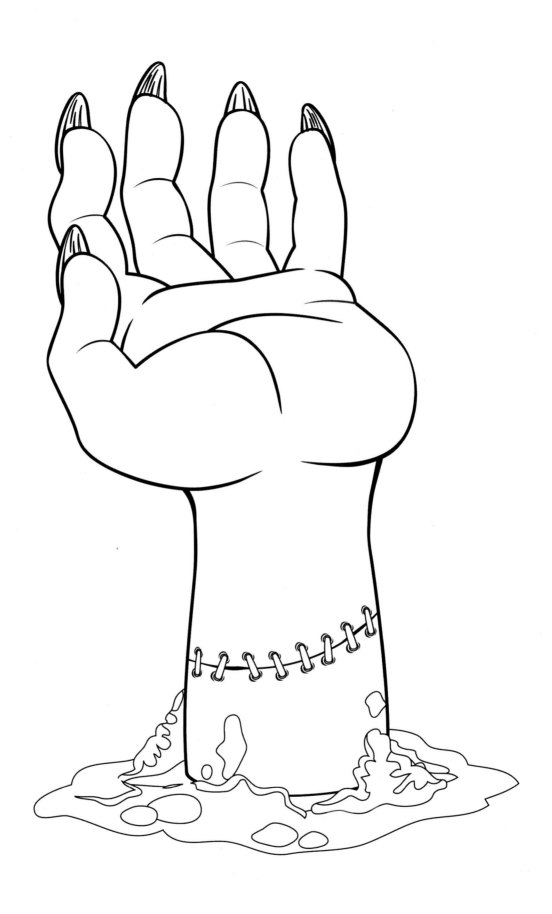

Add some colors to the picture by copying the colors from the next page!

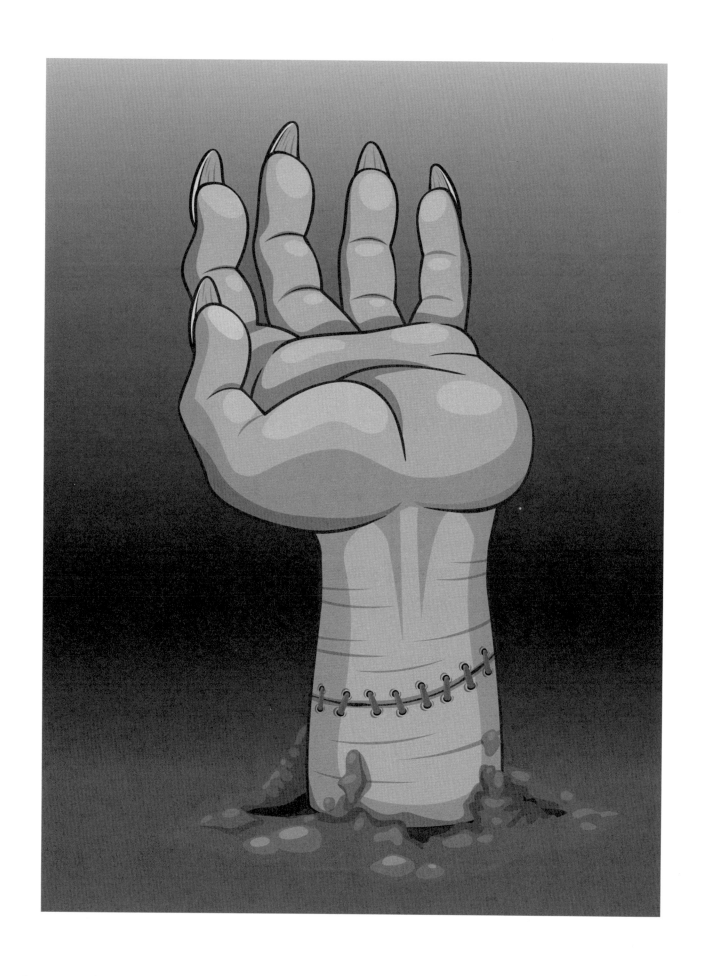

Look at the colors! Make the pictures look the same by copying the colors!

Add some colors to the picture by copying the colors from the next page!

Look at the colors! Make the pictures look the same by copying the colors!

Add some colors to the picture by copying the colors from the next page!

Look at the colors! Make the pictures look the same by copying the colors!

Add some colors to the picture by copying the colors from the next page!

Look at the colors! Make the pictures look the same by copying the colors!

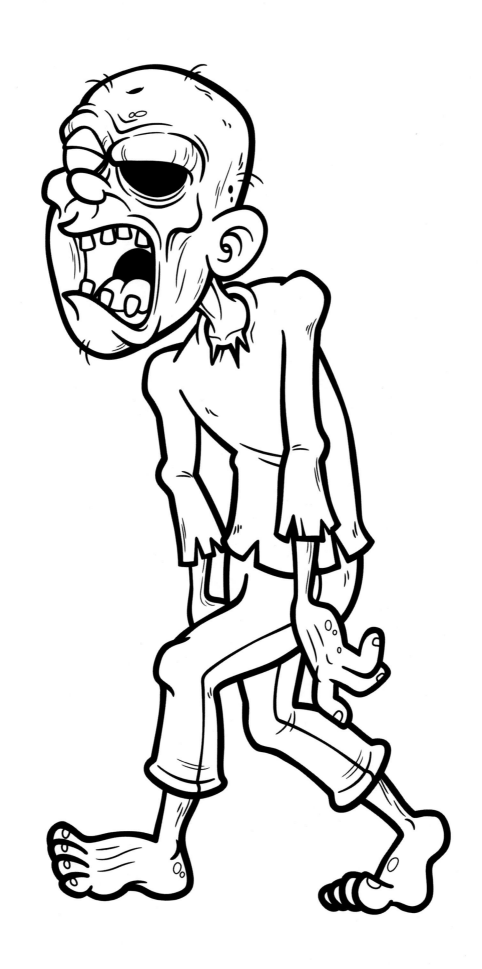

Add some colors to the picture by copying the colors from the next page!

Look at the colors! Make the pictures look the same by copying the colors!

Add some colors to the picture by copying the colors from the next page!

Look at the colors! Make the pictures look the same by copying the colors!

Add some colors to the picture by copying the colors from the next page!

Look at the colors! Make the pictures look the same by copying the colors!

Add some colors to the picture by copying the colors from the next page!

Look at the colors! Make the pictures look the same by copying the colors!

Add some colors to the picture by copying the colors from the next page!

Look at the colors! Make the pictures look the same by copying the colors!

Add some colors to the picture by copying the colors from the next page!

Look at the colors! Make the pictures look the same by copying the colors!

Add some colors to the picture by copying the colors from the next page!

Look at the colors! Make the pictures look the same by copying the colors!

Made in the USA
San Bernardino, CA
30 March 2016